SHIPPING
on the
HUMBER

The South Bank

During the twentieth century, large tonnages of petroleum liquids were carried in tanker barges on the Humber waterways. South bank havens and docks received deliveries, initially from Saltend depot, near Hull, (where jetties were opened in 1914) and, subsequently, mainly from Immingham Oil Terminal (opened in 1969). John Harker Ltd of Knottingley, West Yorkshire, was a major oil carrier in the region, eventually building a fleet of motor barges which allowed the company's activities to reach a peak in the 1950s and 1960s. In the 1920s, however, when the traffic began, craft were usually dumb, i.e. unpowered, and here in 1927 Harkers' *Jim* is making the first delivery to the Shell depot at Brigg. The dumb tanker had been launched from Dunstons' yard at Thorne earlier that year. Its voyage to Brigg from the loading point at Saltend would have involved towage by steam tug up the Humber to Ferriby Sluice, haulage by horse from Ferriby to Coal Dyke End at Brigg, and poling by the crew upriver to the depot. Arrangements for haulage by horse involved a telephone call from Saltend to the lock-keeper at South Ferriby who, because the horse marine lived a couple of miles up the Ancholme, sent him a telegram giving the vessel's estimated time of arrival at the sluice. The marine and horse then tramped down to Ferriby to meet the vessel and tow it upriver. A voyage on the often rough and stormy Humber must have been an uncomfortable experience for the helmsman with no shelter on *Jim's* open deck and this was the case for all sailing craft too. Only when engines were installed did wheelhouses begin to be fitted to some of these craft.

Although no petroleum liquids are now delivered by tanker barges to shore-based tanks on the south bank, oil traffic still exists, with sophisticated tanker barges carrying cargoes from Immingham to wharves alongside the Aire & Calder Navigation in West Yorkshire and to ships needing refuelling at Hull and Immingham. (*Valerie and John Holland Collection*)

SHIPPING
on the
HUMBER

The South Bank

MIKE TAYLOR

TEMPUS

Prior to the Second World War, the Humber was home to both keels and sloops, built of either wood or iron. These sailing craft had almost identical hulls but differed in their sailing gear. Sloops were easier to handle on the tideway and were the workhorses of the south bank with Barton-on-Humber the hub of this activity.

Edward Paget-Tomlinson's drawing of the iron sloop *Nero* shows its fore and aft rig with two large triangular sails. The raised leeboard, visible amidships and on several craft pictured in this book, can be lowered to enable a keel or sloop to 'grip' the water it is sailing on. *Nero's* history is described in Chapter 7.

First published 2003

Tempus Publishing Limited
The Mill, Brimscombe Port,
Stroud, Gloucestershire, GL5 2QG

British Library Cataloguing in Publication Data.
A catalogue record for this book is available from the British Library.

ISBN 0 7524 2780 6

Typesetting and origination by Tempus Publishing Limited
Printed in Great Britain by Midway Colour Print, Wiltshire

Contents

Acknowledgements

The late Ken Straw, Brian Peeps and Stuart Sizer have been most helpful in providing both information and illustrations. The late John Frank, Bernard Hughes, John and Valerie Holland, Garry Crossland, Brian Mummery, Cyril Harrison, Dave Thompson, Clarence Foster, Arthur Credland, David Hill, Les Hill, Roger Foster, Les Reid, Rodney Clapson and Mike Holmes of ABP, Hull, have also responded to my requests for assistance.

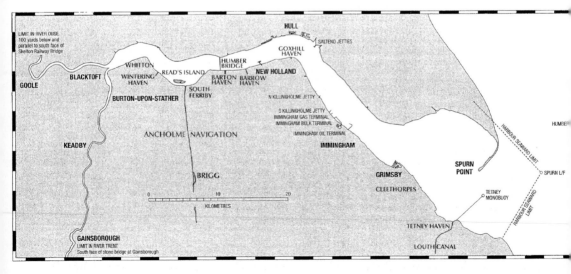

A map showing the docks, havens and rivers of the south bank of the River Humber.

Introduction

The River Humber, formed at the confluence of the Ouse and Trent, once comprised natural tidal havens (harbours) where small rivers had their outlets along its south bank. One larger river, the Ancholme, also joined the Humber along this Lincolnshire shore. Almost all these stretches of water have been used for commercial navigation for centuries with movement upstream taking place during the four hours immediately before high water to use the power of the incoming tide. Craft heading downstream usually leave a berth when there is sufficient water on it to float the vessel and then 'punch' the incoming tide before it turns, and movement is assisted by the ebb.

By the 1900s, docks had been built at Grimsby and New Holland, the port of Immingham was under construction, and both the Ancholme Navigation and Louth Navigation had been cut and developed into what would be their final forms. The Caistor Canal, branching off from the Ancholme, had been opened and had fallen into disuse by this time, and the Louth Navigation was in its final years before being closed in 1923. Barton Haven was still the base of many Humber sloops and New Holland had become established as the south bank base of cross-river passenger ferries. Several cross-river cargo services also existed at one time but, by the middle of the twentieth century, these were in decline and keels and sloops had ceased to sail, usually having been motorised.

The ports of Grimsby and Immingham and the New Holland ferries were nationalised in 1948. Commercial traffic on the Ancholme ended in the early 1970s, whilst the motor barges that replaced the sailing craft steadily declined in numbers for various reasons and only a few petroleum tanker barges and Trent gravellers now remain. Seagoing craft, however, have reversed this downward trend and the Humber Estuary is currently one of the busiest stretches of waterway in Britain.

This book concentrates on the inland waterway craft that brought imported foreign goods and Yorkshire coal to, and took away bricks and raw materials from, the south bank wharves and navigations during the past century; however, shipping has not been ignored, especially the transhipments between seagoing and river craft. Keels, sloops, motor barges, lighters, tugs, pilot boats and cross-river ferries are all featured, together with the Lincolnshire boatyards where many of them were built and/or maintained.

The illustrations include maps and photographs dating from the late nineteenth century to the present time and are arranged topographically in a random chronological order, travelling upriver from the estuary mouth. My own photographs and those from my collection (greatly enhanced by contributions from collections of the late John Frank and the late Ken Straw) are uncredited whilst those provided by the Humber Keel & Sloop Preservation Society (HKSPS) and others are individually acknowledged.

One
Louth to Cleethorpes

The twelve-mile, eight-lock Louth Navigation, fed by the River Lud, was opened throughout in May 1770. During its 150-year lifetime, the terminal basin in Louth, shown in this 1900s view looking north east, saw exports of Lincolnshire corn and wool to inland waterway ports in Yorkshire with craft bringing return cargoes of coal, often loaded at Keadby on the River Trent. At one time, there were five corn merchants, five coal merchants and three timber merchants with premises at Louth's Riverhead; more than at Grimsby. As a centre for the collection and export of local produce and distribution of coal and other imports, Louth had the advantage of being at the hub of several turnpike roads. The Louth-built sloop *Ebenezer,* owned by Richard Nell whose properties surrounded much of the Riverhead, is prominent in the foreground. (*Stuart Sizer Collection*)

This late nineteenth-century photograph of Louth's Riverhead shows a sloop moored by the Navigation Warehouse. Vessels either sailed on the navigation, driven by seamarsh winds, or were towed by horse. Puzzlingly, a square sail characteristic of a Humber keel seems to have been used in this case. (*Stuart Sizer Collection*)

20 May 1920 was a significant day for the Louth Canal because flash floods in the town, in addition to killing twenty-three people, effectively ended its life. Craft were washed down to the first lock as shown in this view looking north east, causing much damage to canal furniture and nearby warehouses. One of the shipyard huts, damaged during the flood, is visible in the centre of the picture. An approximately 12ft x 6ft cog boat, usually towed behind a keel or sloop to be used for many essential navigational operations off the keel as well as a lifeboat in emergencies, is here being used by men to inspect the damage.

LOUTH NAVIGATION.

WARNING.

Notice is hereby given that any person or persons who shall dig into or through the **CANAL BANKS** for the purpose of draining **WATER** from the said Canal or for any other purpose will forthwith be prosecuted.

BY ORDER OF THE COMMISSIONERS.

PORTER WILSON.
CLERK.

Louth, 20th July, 1897.

Parker, Machine Printer, Market-place, Louth.

The Louth Navigation met the tidal waters of the Humber at Tetney Lock which was provided with two pairs of both upper and lower gates so that craft could pass whether the water level in the Humber was above or below that in the canal. In this 1900s view looking north, the sluice lies to the left and the lock to the right. The Crown and Anchor pub is visible amongst the warehouses and lock-keeper's residence. One of the crew may be seen raising or lowering the sail of the sloop-rigged billyboy (a seagoing craft with a hull similar to that of a Humber keel or sloop but fitted with bulwarks) waiting to enter the lock and negotiate the three-mile-long channel through the sand flats into the Humber. The vessel is clinker-built (overlapping planks), a method of construction of wooden craft superseded by carvel-building (abutting planks) early in the twentieth century.

Opposite, above: Several English canals have attracted waterway enthusiasts to form societies dedicated to their welfare and the Louth Navigation is no exception. This postcard, produced by the Louth Navigation Trust, publicises the society by depicting a waterway scene near Louth and by reproducing a typical notice that was affixed to the canal company's properties in the late nineteenth century.

Opposite, below: A characteristic feature of the Louth Navigation's locks was their curved four-section sides with wooden rubbing posts between each 'scollop'; they claimed to give extra strength to the walls in their marshland situation. These are evident in this illustration from the 1900s showing a laden sloop fitted with a bowsprit entering Keddington lock, the seventh and penultimate lock up from Tetney, whilst en route for Louth's Riverhead, half a mile away. (*Stuart Sizer Collection*)

Above: Fishing boats were regular users of the Louth Navigation, making frequent voyages to sell their catches at the 'Fish Shambles' in central Louth. Here, the small sailing vessel *Orient* is waiting outside Tetney Lock's Crown and Anchor, prior to penning out from the canal into the Humber. (*Stuart Sizer Collection*)

Europe's first monobuoy, designed to serve Conoco's Immingham refinery with North Sea crude oil via storage tanks at Tetney, was positioned in the Humber during 1971. Ten years later this was replaced by a more modern buoy which is currently serviced by dedicated shuttle tankers delivering between eighty and ninety-five cargoes, each of about 100,000 tonnes per annum, loaded offshore. 8.5 million tonnes were imported by this means in 2001 and here one of the regular callers, Ugland's *Evita*, is shown moored at the buoy with a tug and workboat in attendance. (*Conoco*)

Opposite, below: The canal was difficult to access for a loaded boat, and one with a draught of 5ft could only pass into or out of Tetney Lock for a total of about eight days each month around the times of the biggest spring tides. Here, the sloop *Sarah* is berthed on the mud below the lock waiting for water. As well as this problem, the Louth Navigation also suffered from a lack of maintenance through most of its lifetime, leading to poor condition of its locks and bridges. Additionally, dredging was never adequate and, when the Great Northern Railway Co. took over the canal's lease in 1847, they ensured that the situation did not improve in a successful attempt to win traffic from the waterway. By the time of the 1920 floods, traffic had almost completely fallen away and repair of the damage caused seemed pointless so the canal was abandoned in 1924. Today, the Louth Navigation is used as a land drain and the tidal limit has been moved a mile downstream with construction of a new drainage sluice. (*Stuart Sizer Collection*)

Harkers' tanker *Newtondale H* left Saltend oil terminal with 480 tonnes of fuel oil bound for Grimsby Docks on a foggy day in the mid-1960s, before such craft were fitted with radar. The skipper turned to head for the dock entrance lock but ran aground and, after the tide had ebbed, found himself stranded on Cleethorpes beach as shown. Fortunately the tanker floated off undamaged on the next tide.

Two
Grimsby Docks

Originally, the port of Grimsby was sited on a haven into which the River Freshney had been diverted in 1790 to reduce silting. The 'Old Dock' and entrance lock, opened in 1800, were then constructed at the Freshney/Humber confluence, west of the present site of the Fish Docks. Half a century later, the Manchester, Sheffield & Lincolnshire Railway Co., who were virtually responsible for creation of the port by investing heavily in its docks and railway facilities, opened another dock projecting further into the Humber and this 1850s painting depicts its construction. This 'New Dock' and its entrance locks opened in 1852 and became Royal Dock in 1854 when Queen Victoria visited the port. In 1872, construction of another dock at 90 degrees to the Old Dock began at its northern end. It was completed by 1879 and both these docks became Alexandra Dock in 1879 after a visit by the future Queen; the original dock becoming the 'South Arm' and the new addition the 'West Arm'.

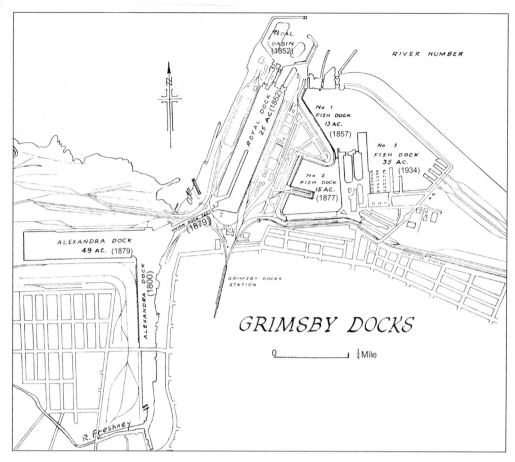

A map of Grimsby Docks in the 1950s. Opening dates of docks are given in brackets, whilst AC indicates their areas in acres. The Royal Dock's two entrance locks had dimensions of 70ft x 300ft and 45ft x 200ft, respectively, and there was a graving dock 70ft x 350ft slightly to the east of and parallel to these locks. By 1879, a cutting (Union Dock) had been made between Royal and Alexandra Docks to allow craft to move directly between them without having to pass out through one entrance lock and in through another. The entrance lock to Alexandra Dock was closed in 1917. During the 1970s, the smaller Royal Dock entrance lock was also closed and the graving dock filled in before being paved over to provide additional open storage space.

This picture dates from the 1930s when Grimsby was the country's premier deep sea fishing port. In 1850, the landing of fish was not of major importance here, but construction by the Manchester, Sheffield & Lincolnshire Railway Co. of a fish dock and the existence of rail links with Manchester and London attracted craft to land their catches. A steam trawler registered in the borough is shown leaving one of the fish dock entrance locks bound for the North Sea fishing grounds. A lifeboat station can be seen to the left of the view.

Originally, coal to fire the fishing fleet's boilers was brought either by inland waterway craft from Yorkshire coalfields or, more usually, loaded from rail-fed drops on the dockside. After the Second World War however, diesel oil was the fuel in demand and this 1979 photograph shows Exnor Craggs' bunkering fleet of tanker barges (left to right, *Strong Hand*, *Good Hand* and *Revillio*) in the fish docks.

TOWER
AND ROYAL DOCK
ENTRANCE,
GRIMSBY

Inland waterway craft are visible amongst the ships in a busy Royal Dock at Grimsby in this view from the 1900s. The port handled cargoes brought to or from it mainly along its rail links, but at this time there was some transhipment to inland waterway craft of bar iron, timber and sugar bound for the West Riding of Yorkshire.

Tugs, barges and shipping are shown moored in Royal Dock in the 1950s with rail-fed coal drops in the background.

Opposite: This postcard view across the Royal Dock tidal basin features a dredging plant designed to work in the docks and its approaches, but is dominated by a campanile, the 309ft-high Dock Tower, 28ft square at its base, completed in 1852. The structure stands on an 'island' between the two Royal Dock entrance locks. The reservoir 247ft up the tower held 30,000 gallons of water, originally used for operating lock gates and machinery around the dock estate. A new hydraulic system was installed in 1900, making this function obsolete and it is now merely a landmark visible on most photographs of the docks.

This early-1920s aerial view, looking north east over the southern arm of Grimsby's Alexandra Dock, shows the 1873-built Corporation Road swing bridge with inland waterway craft, some loaded with grain from Hull, clustered outside William Marshall's 1906-built Victoria Mill nearby. Spillers later took over the mill; however, over twenty years ago it was converted into residential apartments.

Opposite, above: Workboats in Grimsby's Royal Dock in the late 1950s gather around the sunken tug *Lady Cecilia* with only the tip of its funnel visible above the water. The tug had been tied up tightly against the coaling jetty, but water flooded in through an open hatch after the vessel tilted when the level in the dock rose. The owners are rumoured to have tried to raise the vessel themselves by sucking water out of the vessel's funnel! (*Lincoln & Hull Marine Contractors*)

Opposite, below: After the tug owners' vain attempts to raise the vessel, Lincoln & Hull Marine Contractors were called in. They moored an empty barge on each side of the sunken tug and bridged the gap between the barges with steel beams. Steel wires were then eased beneath the tug and it was lifted bodily to the surface. *Lady Cecilia* is shown after being raised. (*Lincoln & Hull Marine Contractors*)

The 60ft x 15ft motor tanker barge *Tetney* (built at Beverley in 1909 by Cook, Welton & Gemmell for the Tetney Oil & Marine Co. of Grimsby and originally steam-powered) is shown sometime after its 1917 sale to the Anglo-American Oil Co., passing beneath the raised span of Corporation Road Lift Bridge. This was built in 1928 to replace the original swing bridge across Alexandra Dock. *Tetney* delivered to both Barton and Brigg during its lifetime. The vessel was broken up in 1956. (*Esso* magazine)

Starting in the late nineteenth century, Nelson Blow & Co. provided a Hull-Grimsby cargo service with their steam barges *Basalt* and *Quenast*, each fitted with a steam winch and derrick. *Basalt* (a 72ft x 15ft steel vessel built by Warrens of New Holland in 1905) is shown handling a cargo of general goods on 'Blows' Landing' at Grimsby's Riverhead (the southern extremity of Alexandra Dock) in the 1920s with a dray in attendance. These craft also towed the company's lighters across carrying flour in sacks from Ranks' Mill at Hull.

A 1934 advertisement for Blow's Hull and Grimsby Steamers.

Blow's *Quenast* (74ft long and built at Beverley in 1895) is shown discharging goods brought from Oberon Wharf at Hull to a horse-drawn cart. This view of their landing at Grimsby's Riverhead was taken from the town's Victoria Street in 1919. A loaded sloop with plank ashore lies off Dawber, Townsley & Co.'s wharf, probably waiting to discharge bricks brought from Ferriby Sluice on the Ancholme Navigation.

24

Oil seeds transhipped in Hull's docks were delivered to Sowerby & Co.'s Mill at Riverhead by Blow's and Spillers' barges and this view from the 1930s shows such a cargo being discharged at the mill by bucket elevator.

Passenger services across the Humber were augmented in 1969 by a daily hovercraft service of six twenty-minute round trips, though it lasted for only eight months. The two craft, *Mercury* and *Minerva*, seemed to be flimsily constructed and suffered almost daily breakdowns before being withdrawn from service. *Mercury* is shown after leaving the Queen's Steps outside Grimsby's Royal Dock for Minerva Pier, Hull, a short distance above Corporation Pier, in February 1969. (*Grimsby Evening Telegraph*)

Opposite, above: In an operation similar to that of Blows, the Grimsby Express Packet Co. provided a cross-Humber goods service operated by a pair of craft throughout the first two thirds of the twentieth century. Initially the vessels were steam powered, but by the 1950s, when this advertisement was published, they had been converted to diesel power. The photograph was taken at the company's Grimsby depot in Alexandra Dock; their Hull depot was at Blackfriars Wharf, close to the present Myton Bridge across 'The Harbour' (a term used to describe the lower reaches of the River Hull).

Opposite, below: Immediately before to the Second World War, the steam barges *Trent* (100ft x 20ft, built for the company in 1931 by Dunstons of Thorne) and *W.N.* (90ft x 18ft, built in 1909 by Warrens of New Holland for W. Nettleton of Hull) were being used by the Grimsby Express Packet Co. They carried miscellaneous cargoes such as nets, weights, ropes, fruit, vegetables, titanium oxide and imported butter across the Humber between Grimsby and Hull. As with Blow's service, lighters were frequently towed across, often these were vessels owned by Spillers or Leethams loaded with cargoes of grain for Grimsby's Victoria Mills. The photograph, taken in the early 1970s when both *Trent* and *W.N* had been fitted with diesel engines, shows the two vessels waiting to load in King George Dock, Hull. (*David Hill*)

Shipbuilding at Grimsby took place outside the docks on the Humber bank between the Royal and Alexandra Docks entrances. Most notable was the J.S. Doig Co. which acquired premises adjacent to the Alexandra Dock entrance lock, building and maintaining mainly fishing vessels and Naval craft during their 1906-1964 existence. The company sold out to the Ross Group who closed the yard in 1969. The 'winged' barge shown was used to keep the water frontage of the shipyards free from silt. It was pushed by water sluiced from Alexandra Dock and winched back with wings folded using a kedge anchor. (*APB*)

In the late nineteenth and early twentieth centuries, paddle steamer excursions were offered from Royal Dock Pier to Hull, South Ferriby and Burton Stather using the Gainsborough United Steam Packet Co.'s *Atlanta* and *Isle of Axholme*. The latter is shown here at the Trentside landing stage at Burton Stather around the turn of the century. In the 1970s, British Railways' Humber ferries also made summer excursions from here and from elsewhere.

Three
Immingham: its Dock and River Jetties

In the 1900s, a new dock was planned for Grimsby. On the Dock Engineer's advice it was built at Immingham, close to the Humber's deep water channel a few miles upstream. Advance publicity featured several 'aerial view' drawings which were published as postcards and this one shows the dock, graving dock, railway-fed coaling hoists, entrance lock able to accommodate any vessel able to transit the Suez Canal, and its east and west jetties.

This is another of the six pre-opening postcards featuring drawings of Immingham Dock. (The other four appeared in Tempus Publishing's *Immingham and the Great Central Legacy* by Brian Mummery and Ian Butler.) Although a tug and lighter are depicted to the left of the scene, such traffic was less in evidence here than at older Humber ports, Immingham Dock having been designed to specialise in the export of rail-delivered coal. The reverse of the card states, 'View of SEVEN COAL HOISTS capable of shipping five thousand tons per hour. Accommodation for 11,600 loaded wagons. 170 miles of sidings.'

In July 1906, the first sod of the future Immingham Dock was cut by Lady Henderson, wife of the Chairman of the Great Central Railway Co. (GCRC), formerly the Manchester, Sheffield & Lincolnshire Railway Co. Early stages of the construction work are shown on what were previously green fields. (*The Immingham Museum*)

Construction of the entrance lock to Immingham Dock is shown in this 1910 photograph, with the outer and middle gates in position. (*The Immingham Museum*)

FIRST VESSEL TO ENTER
IMMINGHAM DOCK.

This photograph was taken in May 1912 before the official opening of Immingham Dock. It commemorates the Stockholm-registered SS *Max*, dressed overall and handled by the GCR's tug *Central* No.1, becoming the first ship to enter the newly-built dock.

The GCR's Hull to New Holland ferry *Killingholme* brought King George V and Queen Mary from Grimsby to officially open Immingham Dock in July 1912. The paddle steamer with its royal party is shown preparing to tie up, with troops waiting at the ready on the eastern wall of the dock. The vessel, unusually with steering gear both fore and aft, was built by Earles of Hull and had been launched only a few months earlier. The dock was named 'King's Dock' but only recently has this name entered common usage.

The GCRC's Grimsby & Immingham Electric Railway linking the new dock to its parent town was opened in 1912 to carry dockers to and from the port of Immingham. The lines were very busy at times of shift changes. This photograph, dating from after 1923 when the London & North Eastern Railway had absorbed the GCR, shows one of the tramcars used. The system closed in 1961.

ENTRANCE TO KINGS DOCK, IMMINGHAM. 1.

The *Hebble* was salvaged by removing some of its superstructure and welding two 25ft steel towers to the then vertical deck with the ship in the position shown. Water was admitted to the dock in early March as two railway locomotives began to pull on the towers and within hours the vessel had been righted. (*The Immingham Museum*)

Opposite, above: During the First and Second World Wars, Immingham provided a convenient base for the Royal Navy. In the First World War, keels and sloops were chartered both to transport stores from the dock to naval vessels at anchor in the estuary and bought for service on continental waterways. A fleet of submarines and fast patrol boats were based here at the time and E-class submarines may be seen preparing to leave the dock entrance lock with craft visible in the graving dock beyond.

Opposite, below: Exceptionally high tides at the end of January 1953 flooded Immingham graving dock with the results shown. The Swedish ship SS *Hedja* remained afloat, the Trinity House light vessel *Varne* filled and turned over, and the Associated Humber Lines' SS *Hebble* was lifted off the dock bottom before rolling over to smash its superstructure on the dockside. (*The Immingham Museum*)

The righted *Hebble* is shown in Immingham dry dock on 12 March. After a complete refit, the ship was back in service on its owners' Goole-Antwerp service by September, finally being withdrawn in May 1959. (*The Immingham Museum*)

The SS *Coracero* is shown moored at the Mineral Quay in Immingham Dock loading steel billets for Buenos Aires from inland waterway craft in 1964. (*ABP*)

Opposite, below: Sulphur from the USA is here being transhipped from ship to inland waterway craft at Immingham Dock in the 1950s. The cargo was taken to Laporte Titanium's factory at Stallingborough, a couple of miles away, where it was converted into sulphuric acid to be used in the production of the white pigment titanium dioxide.

A modern aerial view, looking east, of Immingham Dock and its jetties, built to handle ships too big or too deep in the water to enter the dock. From top to bottom, the jetties are: Immingham Oil Terminal (opened 1969), Eastern Jetty, Western Jetty (both built at the same time as the dock), Immingham Bulk Terminal (opened 1970) and Immingham Gas Jetty (opened 1985). (*ABP*)

Opposite: Cargo is being discharged in 1960 from the MV *Kallada* into barges, including G.D. Holmes's *Evelyn*, at Immingham Dock's Fisons' Quay. From the early 1950s until the 1970s, this barge company loaded large tonnages of both sulphur and ilmenite at Immingham for delivery to Laporte Titanium's jetty at Stallingborough and some of the sulphur to chemical works on the Aire & Calder Navigation at Castleford. (*ABP*)

39

One of the largest tankers to arrive at the Immingham Oil Terminal in the 1980s was *World Brasilia* which discharged a part-cargo of crude oil weighing 103,440 tonnes. Associated Petroleum Terminals (APT) claim that each year they handle 3,000 vessels here and 25 million tonnes of oil and petroleum products over the three-jetty, nine-berth complex. (*ABP*)

This view from the bridge of a supertanker at Immingham Oil Terminal illustrates the huge width of such a ship. (*ABP*)

The first vessel of over 300,000 tonnes deadweight to enter the Humber was the *Golar Edinburgh* which delivered a part-cargo of 120,000 tonnes of Iranian crude oil in 1996. The 1082ft x 190ft vessel had a draught of 40ft with a clearance in places of only 5ft beneath its hull. (*ABP*)

J.H. Pigott & Son commenced towage at Grimsby in the nineteenth century and extended their services to Immingham in 1956 (their *Lady Cecilia* is shown on page 20). They remained a family firm until 1973 when they were taken over by United Towing and subsequently became Humber Tugs when purchased by the Howard Smith Co. in 1987. As Humber Tugs, five new craft were built, all maintaining the *Lady-* naming pattern and all delivered in 1991. All five tugs have occasionally been used together to berth some of the large bulk carriers that visit Immingham. They are shown here, from left: *Lady Josephine, Lady Cecilia, Lady Sarah, Lady Kathleen, Lady Anya.* (*Humber Tugs*)

Here's half the story

Howard Smith Towage

for the full picture on the Humber

Humber Tugs began to operate as Howard Smith Towage in 1996. This advertisement from 2000 seems to cry out for an aerial photograph instead of the one shown. The company became Adsteam in 2001 when the Adelaide Steamship Co. bought out their fellow Australian company. (*Howard Smith Towage*)

Ships have been piloted when voyaging on the river to and from Humber ports, including those on the south bank, for centuries. In 1895, a steam pilot cutter was introduced onto the Humber to replace the sailing schooners previously used to transfer pilots to and from ships. This provided a floating base for the pilots at the estuary mouth. The cutter shown was built by Earles of Hull in 1931 and named *J.H. Fisher* after the Chairman of the Humber Conservancy. Small wooden motorised boarding boats to transport the pilots were kept aboard the cutter and one may be seen in use. (*ABP*)

The pilot cutter/boarding boat system was retained until 1972 when high-speed glass fibre pilot launches were introduced on the river. *Humber Tartan* is shown at speed in the 1990s, delivering a pilot to a ship in the estuary. (*ABP*)

Tankers owned by John H. Whitaker leaving, loading and arriving at Immingham Oil Jetty in 1979.

Nowadays, Immingham is usually busy with shipping and there is great demand for fuel oil as bunkers for seagoing vessels. Here in 1999, a tanker owned by Rix Petroleum, *Rix Osprey*, is seen delivering such a cargo with one of Whitakers' tanker barges in the background carrying out similar work. (*Rix Petroleum*)

Above: In the mid-1990s the LASH (Lighter Aboard Ship) system of transporting barges containing cargoes by use of a mother ship returned to the Humber. An experiment with them in 1974 ended in failure when Hull dockers refused to cooperate. This time, the semi-submersible ship *Spruce*, seen moored at Immingham's Eastern Jetty in 2001, brought LASH barges from Rotterdam where the much larger mother ship had discharged them and the operation has run smoothly for several years.

Right: Within four hours of arrival, *Spruce* has been lowered into the water so that tugs can remove the barges it has brought and this process is shown under way. Tugs then take them to their destinations along the inland waterways. Imports are mainly rice for Selby and timber; exports are chiefly steel.

In the First World War, the paddle steamer *Killingholme*, which participated in the opening of Immingham Dock, was used out in the Humber handling seaplanes based at Killingholme, being torpedoed whilst doing so. In the Second World War, it served as a tender to barges commandeered as tethering bases for barrage balloons designed to obstruct enemy aircraft. Such a barge is shown on the Humber together with its balloon in the 1940s.

Four
New Holland

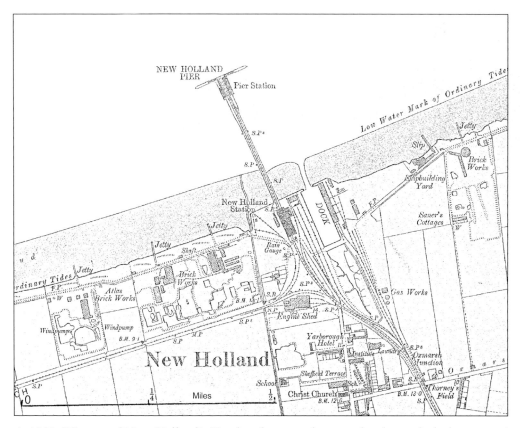

A 1908 OS map of New Holland's Humber frontage showing the shipyard, dock, pier and several brickworks' jetties.

Few photographs seem to exist of shipbuilding, launchings and repairing at Warrens' boatyard which specialised in steel craft and began in 1899 on the site of the GCR's boat-building yard, ending about 1960. Six illustrations have been included here to feature Warrens-built craft at various points on the Humber waterways. Built in 1911 for the Goole & Sheffield Transport Co. and designed to work up to Doncaster on the Sheffield & South Yorkshire Navigation, the steam tug *Clara Marion* is shown in Stainforth Basin in the 1920s.

Left: The Humber Keel & Sloop Preservation Society's *Comrade* was constructed in 1923 as the Sheffield size (61½ ft x 15½ ft) keel *Wanda*. The vessel became *Comrade* in 1929 and its first engine was installed in 1933. In 1974, *Comrade* was sold to the HKSPS to be restored and re-rigged and is shown here with mainsail and topsail raised on the Humber in the late 1970s. A keel's mast was stepped further aft than that of a sloop. Most sailing craft depicted in this book are sloops. (*H. Byers*)

Above: Clarence T,
built by Warrens for
J.J. Tomlinson as a
sloop in 1925, is
shown in Sheffield
Basin as a motor
barge delivering
grain to the silo in
the 1960s.

Right: Green One, was
built in 1932 by
Warrens as a Trent
size (82½ ft x 14½ ft)
dumb barge for Trent
Carriers. It was
subsequently
motorised and is
shown tied up on the
River Hull below
Beverley waiting for
water to enable it to
continue its voyage
further upriver.
(David Hill)

The Trent size motor tug/barge *Greendale* was built by Warrens in 1932 for Trent Carriers and is shown here with dumb barges and Trent detergent foam in Stoke Bardolph Lock during the 1960s whilst returning to Hull from Nottingham.

Tees, a Trent-size towing barge was built by Warrens for the Trent Navigation Co. in 1932 and is seen rising in Newark Town Lock in the 1950s when ownership had passed to the British Transport Commission.

In 1970, Warrens' yard began building craft again under the ownership of New Holland Shipyard. Its first vessel, the 149ft x 20ft motor barge *Phoenix*, a Trent graveller subsequently named *Carimor*, was launched in July 1972. It is seen heading up the Trent beneath Keadby Bridge in the 1980s to collect a load of aggregate.

The motor barge *Swinderby*, 150ft x 28ft with a capacity of 750 tonnes, was built in the 1970s at New Holland Shipyard for Lincoln & Hull Water Transport as a Trent graveller. Here it has been used in early 1979 to carry a 100ft stair tower, constructed at Barton-upon-Humber, into Hull's Alexandra Dock for transhipment and onward delivery by coaster to Sullom Voe. (*Lincoln & Hull Marine Contractors*)

The New Holland yard also did some shipbreaking. *Carimor* is shown leaving the River Hull in the 1980s, with Whitakers' tanker *Sirwin* fastened alongside to cross the Humber and deliver it to the yard to be scrapped.

New Holland Dock was situated just above the shipyard. Tugs, barges and lighters may be seen on this postcard view of it dating from the 1910s. At this time, coal brought by rail was used to bunker the GCR's tugs based both here, at Grimsby and at Immingham, using the chute to the left. Five or six barge loads were also carried across the Humber each day to fuel trawlers in the fish docks at this time.

From 1848, a Hull-New Holland Dock lighter service was provided to link with trains on the south bank serving New Holland. Cargoes from Hull were loaded both in the docks and from the warehouses on the River Hull's Lime Kiln Creek, shown here in 1908 when operated by the GCRC. The lighters were towed across the Humber by tugs. Later, the service operated out of Hull's Railway Dock.

The Hull-New Holland Dock lighter service utilised the warehouse on the eastern side of the dock, as shown here in the 1940s, with lighters owned by the LNER at this time. The service ended in 1960. (*Brian Peeps Collection*)

The east side of New Holland Dock is still in use, though the west side is obviously silted up. The ship *Sarah* is shown in 2002 discharging a cargo of steel here onto the former site of the lighter service sheds.

In the eighteenth and early nineteenth centuries, the Humber supported a large number of cross-river passenger ferries but the Hull-New Holland service began to dominate the scene from 1849 when the railway came to the Lincolnshire port. Here, the paddle steamer *Cleethorpes*, which worked on the service between 1903 and 1934, is moored at the floating jetty adjoining Victoria (Corporation) Pier at the Hull end of the operation. (It was named Victoria after the Queen left from here for Grimsby in 1854.) Promenades were added to the pier in 1882 and demolished in 1965.

With *Cleethorpes* astern, the paddle steamer *Grimsby* is shown moored at the east slope of New Holland Pier in the 1900s. *Grimsby* worked on the Hull-New Holland service between 1888 and 1924. In the early 1920s, the ferry service was carrying between 25,000 and 30,000 passengers, 250 vehicles, 12,000 animals (sheep or cattle) and 500 tonnes of bagged goods per week!

To minimise delays in loading and unloading at low water (a crane and cradle on the pier were once used to handle vehicles at this state of the tide), a floating pier pontoon was built for New Holland by Goole Shipbuilders in 1936. It is shown being delivered by the tug *Autocrat* and remained in service until the ferries finished in 1981.

The coal-fired paddle steamer *Lincoln Castle* is pictured leaving New Holland for the twenty-minute voyage to Hull with the top of the floating pier clearly visible. This vessel was the last coal-fired paddle steamer to be in regular service in Britain until it failed a boiler test in 1978 and was withdrawn.

Lincoln Castle, away from the Hull-New Holland ferry service, is seen on an enthusiasts' cruise on the River Ouse after passing into British Railways' ownership. When on the move, the stoker and almost all the moving machinery were on view and this, plus the smell of oil and steam, made for a memorable experience. Surprisingly, the two paddles on each of these three *Castles* could not be rotated independently, causing a lack of manoeuvrability of the vessels; skilful use of the river's tidal flow was necessary to turn them.

today's cruise

Grimsby, our destination this afternoon - once a busy centre of the
Humber Ferry Service - is now only visited by the occasional cruise,
today we are reviving what was a most popular pastime in the 19th.
century.
Many of our passengers will be boarding the P.S.Lincoln Castle at
New Holland, a township which was built specifically for the Humber
Ferry Service to Hull, previous ferry services using the shorter
run between Barton upon Humber and Hessle. The pier at New Holland,
standing well out into the Humber,is unique in having a Rail
connection so far from land. The pier is owned by British Rail.
The pier at Hull, owned by the City Council, is a much shorter
version, both piers having a floating pontoon of similar design for
vehicle access to the ferry boats. These pontoons were built in
1934, when the Lincoln Castle's sister ships - Tattershall Castle
and Wingfield Castle - came into service. Passengers from New
Holland will have an excellent view of the twin towers of the
Humber Bridge being built on the North Bank at Hessle. If one is
joining the cruise at Hull, a glimpse to stern as we move off will
show how near to the City the bridge will be.
Moving off downstream we pass the mouth of the River Hull and on
past the Eastern Docks of the City. After passing the village of
Paull with its small white Lighthouse (no longer used as such),the
main shipping channel takes us diagonally across the wide estuary
towards the South Bank and the large dockland area of Immingham.
Here we can see the large tankers and commercial ships which visit
this port. Notice here a smell of the sea and how the river has
become more green, having left the muddy waters behind. The North
Bank,at this point,seems to be very distant with its very low lying
land at Sunk Island. Providing the weather is clear,Spurn Point
Lighthouse should be visible to the North East,but more imposing is
the Grimsby Docks Tower, as we enter our Port of Call.On disembarking
it will be noticed we are in the heart of dockland near to the
Royal Dock.
Buses have been provided for a free trip through Grimsby and on to
the neighbouring resort of Cleethorpes and it is from here we
should see Spurn Point across the very mouth of the Humber Estuary.
Time is allowed for a short stroll along the promenade past the
Flower Beds or in the other direction for a plate of cockles or
whelks, perhaps a cup of tea and some candy floss for the youngsters.
All too soon it is time for our buses to return to the Paddle
Steamer for a relaxing journey upstream and home.

The Humber Paddle Steamer Group was formed in April 1973 and hoped to retain one of the
steam ferries in working condition. The Group was dissolved at the end of 1976, having
concluded there was no hope of winning sufficient financial support. The text shown was taken
from a programme provided for participants on a May 1974 cruise from New Holland to
Grimsby via Hull organised by the HPSG. (*Andy Horn Collection*)

An aerial view of New Holland Pier dating from 1974 shortly after the diesel electric paddle steamer *Farringford* (left) had arrived from the Lymington-Yarmouth (IOW) crossing to replace *Wingfield Castle* on the Hull-New Holland ferry service. *Farringford*, unattractive to enthusiasts due to its diesel engine and lack of funnel, worked the very last run of the service on 24 June 1981. The other ferry is *Lincoln Castle*. A walk along the 500yd-long pier between the ferry and the car park in the rain with a cold north-east wind blowing was one of life's discomforts. New Holland Dock may be seen to the left of this view, the shipyard is out of shot further to the left.

Above: On the opening of the Humber Bridge in June 1981, the ferry service ended, New Holland Bulk Services took over the jetty on the Lincolnshire bank at New Holland and converted it to handle freight cargoes. The motor barge *Joyce Hawksley* is shown loading imported palm kernels in July 1986 as *Littondale* and *Deighton* wait.

Left: An aerial view of the jetty from the south bank in 1995 showing the extent of Hew Holland Bulk Services' operation. (*New Holland Bulk Services*)

Five
Barrow and Barton Havens

South bank havens at Goxhill, Barrow, Barton and Winteringham all had a 'market boat' service to Hull. Here, a cargo of sacks of grain is being transferred by mast and derrick from the Barrow market sloop *Toft Newton* to a motor lorry in 1931. (*HKSPS*)

A feature of small shipyards at Barrow, Barton, South Ferriby and Winteringham was the presence of floating dry docks, shown here at J.W.& R. Day's boatyard in Barrow Haven. Craft were admitted at high water with the dock on the riverbed and supported on blocks as the tide ebbed away. One end was then sealed and the whole assembly floated on the next tide, enabling work to be done below the waterline of its occupant. (*HKSPS*)

The floating dry dock is in use in this atmospheric view looking up Barrow Haven taken from Days' boatyard as a steam engine hauls its coaches westwards along the single track railway towards Barton. The line was built by the Manchester, Sheffield & Lincolnshire Railway Co. and opened in 1849. (*Brian Peeps Collection*)

Looking east over Barrow Haven, an aerial view dating from the 1950s, with craft at Days' boatyard for both repairs and breaking up. Fosters' Old Ferry Brickyard with its flooded quarries and a steam passenger train are also visible. The boatyard, established early in the twentieth century on land purchased from Fosters, closed shortly after the photograph was taken. (*Alan Foster*)

Barrow Haven is now the base of Wm. Foster & Sons' timber terminal and MV *Ladoga-102* is pictured here in 1989 after discharging a cargo of Russian timber. The ship was built at a Finnish yard in 1988 and, in addition to sea voyages, was used on the inland waterways of Eastern Europe, such as the Saimaa Lakes and Russian rivers above St Petersburg. (*Alan Foster*)

Since the late nineteenth century, Earles' Cement Co. have manufactured Portland cement at Wilmington, 1½ miles up the River Hull. Clay, one of the essential raw materials for the process, was quarried a short distance west of Barrow, loaded at the company's dock and brought across the Humber. Earles' *Thistle* is shown heading into Hull Harbour in the 1910s on this traffic. These wooden sloops were gradually replaced by steel sloops during the 1920s, the company operating a fleet of five craft in the 1930s. *Southampton*, a fifty-gun retired warship, used since 1868 for training young seamen, is visible to the right.

The 68ft x 17½ft sloop *Miss Madeline* was one of the steel sloops which replaced the wooden craft in Earles' clay-carrying fleet (*Miss Patricia* was another). The vessel was built for the company by Warrens in November 1925 and delivered many cargoes of about 150 tonnes to the works at Wilmington. Motorised in 1948, enabling it to tow dumb craft to its owners' wharf, and lengthened to 88ft in 1970; it was eventually sold to Gainsborough Shipping, then to John Dean and, finally, to Waddingtons of Swinton. *Miss Madeline* is shown here in the 1970s waiting to load coal at Parkhill Colliery staithe on the Aire & Calder Navigation, near Wakefield.

Annual sloop races were held on the Humber until the First World War and were restarted after cessation of hostilities. Wooden sloops were given a half-hour start on steel vessels over a course depending on tides but usually from Barton to off Grimsby and back. The last such race took place in 1929 and this photograph shows the start off Barton Haven.

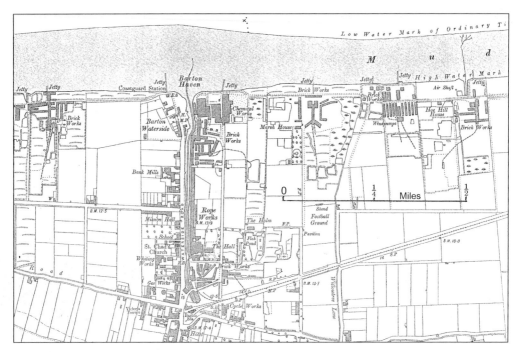

A 1908 OS map of Barton Haven and the Humber foreshore in the area showing several brickworks' jetties as well as the one belonging to the 'chemical works' owned by the Farmers' Co.

The Farmers' Co. had a wooden jetty stretching out into the Humber to the east of Barton Haven from their fertiliser works, established in 1874, and here, a cargo is being discharged by barrow and basket along it from vessels standing on berths that have almost dried out. Coal was one of the commodities imported here but the Farmers' Co. also brought in thousands of tons of copper ore annually to this jetty to be 'burnt' in banks of furnaces and converted into sulphuric acid. Phosphates were also shipped in, together with an occasional load of animal bones, for grinding into bonemeal to produce superphosphate fertiliser by treatment with the acid. A loaded vessel arriving on an incoming tide would be moored at the end of the jetty, head into the tide with anchors out fore and aft on the outside and a rope to the anchor buried inside and to the west of the jetty. (*HKSPS*)

Opposite, below: This clay tile and brickyard, owned and operated by William Blyth & Co., is situated near the eastern edge of the above map at Hoe Hill and is still in business. The Humber bank between New Holland and Barton, together with the lowest mile of the River Ancholme, was once the UK's major producer of roofing tiles with the number of yards in the 1900s running well into double figures. The jetties shown on the map were used to import coal by keel from South and West Yorkshire collieries and to export finished products to Grimsby, Hull or Gainsborough, usually by sloop.

67

Craft coming to load at the jetty usually arrived at high water when the structure was underwater, so they dropped anchor a short distance upriver and waited for the ebb before drifting down onto the jetty. The sloop *Burgate* is shown fouling the jetty in the 1930s after what was probably an error on the captain's part. A concrete jetty was built in the 1950s to replace the structure shown and coasters then called here regularly. Production at the site ended in 1988 after ownership by a number of companies. (*HKSPS*)

Before the New Holland-Hull passenger ferry service had assumed dominance, there were several other similar services such as Grimsby-Hull, Barton-Hull, Barton-Hessle, South Ferriby-Hull and Winteringham-Brough. This 1801 painting, looking towards the Hessle shore, shows ferry boats in Barton Haven.

Opposite, below: Rope from Hall's Barton Ropery, established in 1787, is shown in this photograph dating from 1902 having been hauled by horse and dray to the market boat landing. The boat seems to be being unloaded at this time to another horse and dray. On occasions, one of the market boats came up the haven to collect a large cargo for export from or deliver a bulky load to the ropeworks using a wharf adjacent to the swing footbridge across the haven close to the company's despatch depot. Three sloops lie at anchor in the Humber off Barton Haven. (*HKSPS*)

In addition to owning and operating the Barrow market boat *Toft Newton*, W. Stamp & Son also worked three wooden sloops on the Hull-Barton market boat service in the late nineteenth century and first half of the twentieth century. *Rising Hope* (built Thorne, 1898), *Ever Ready* (built Barton, 1908) and *Rosalie Stamp* (built Barton, 1911) did most voyages. Every day before the First World War, one vessel left the Horsewash, just downstream of Corporation Pier at Hull four hours before high water, bound for Barton and another left Barton Haven for Hull on the first of the ebb. Full cargoes could only be carried on spring tides. A mast and derrick plus hand-wound winch was used for loading and unloading goods.

With Gilstrap, Earp & Co.'s maltings in the background across Barton Haven, workmen handling a market boat pose for a photograph at Stamps' Wharf in the 1900s. (*HKSPS*)

Opposite, above: This view, dating from 1935, features the discharge of goods brought by market sloop from Hull to a horse-drawn dray at Stamps' Landing in Barton Haven, under the watchful eyes of boatmen from craft moored beyond. Deliveries to surrounding towns and villages were still being made by this means at the time. The Hull Brewery Co. still brought their beer to Lincolnshire by market boat and the ropery continued to use the service to carry imported hemp, sisal and coir to their Barton site, whilst local nurserymen used the boat to get their produce to Hull markets. Shortly after this photograph was taken, Stamps purchased a motor lorry and horses were phased out of the operation. The loss of brewery traffic after a takeover and the substitution of traditional materials by man-made fibres at the ropeworks were significant factors in the cessation of the market boats in the 1960s. (*HKSPS*)

The market boat *Ever Ready* frozen in alongside the maltings at Barton Haven in early 1940. The maltings were demolished in 1971. (*HKSPS*)

Across from the market boat landing at Barton Haven, a bagged cargo is being unloaded at another Farmers' Co. wharf in the early 1930s from a keel moored above the maltings. The usual labour-intensive method involving mast and derrick plus barrows and planks is being used. Generally, bagged cargoes for use in the manufacture of fertilisers were discharged here, whilst bulk cargoes were dealt with at the jetty shown on pages 67 and 68. (*HKSPS*)

Opposite, below: Wielding the tools of their trade, workmen at the boatyard which became owned by Clapson & Sons (Shipbuilders) on that company's formation in 1912, pose for the camera inside one of the many wooden carvel-constructed sloops built there. The girder visible would probably have been fabricated at Scunthorpe to become the keelson of the vessel under construction.

The sloop *Mafeking* is ready for its launching into Barton Haven in May 1900 from Brown & Clapson's boatyard on the west bank. The boat builders were established here in 1883 on the site of an earlier yard. All craft were built to be launched end-on at the yard despite the width of water at the top of the tide being only slightly larger than the vessel's length.

The frame of *Peggy*, the last sloop to be built at Clapsons when it was launched in 1935, is shown standing on the havenside with the maltings visible across the water. Clapsons acquired premises at South Ferriby in 1967 and, for a time, worked both yards. They eventually left Barton in the 1980s, after completion of their final building order, to concentrate on the Ancholme site. The company are still in business there.

The smaller of two floating dry docks at Clapsons' here holds a sloop. The other dry dock was constructed in 1911 from a wooden ex-dredger pontoon condemned as unfit for further service and remained in use until the 1970s. Clapsons built two minesweepers during the First World War and six minesweepers plus thirteen fleet tenders during the Second World War. (*HKSPS*)

Local historian and South Ferriby lock-keeper, Ken Straw, captioned this postcard view of Clapsons' yard at Barton Haven thus: 'The wooden barge (ex-keel) is *Kathleen* of Thorne and the two small craft seen over its starboard bow are *Karma* and Aniline. Both these were ex-steamers built of steel and then owned by Wm. Stamp who used them as Barton-Hull market boats; perhaps the last market boats in the area. The vessel in the floating dry dock to the left is one of the 'Cliff Boats', possibly *Adlingfleet*, used for stoning the river banks.'

Looking up Barton Haven at low water from the western bank opposite the former site of Clapsons' yard, now occupied by Offshore Steel Boats, the ex sloop *Phyllis* and lighter *R 35* are shown in 2002 undergoing restoration.

William Foster & Sons' steel sloop *Zenitha*, built by Warrens in 1925, is shown bringing a cargo of South Yorkshire coal from Hatfield, near Doncaster, up Barton Haven on a spring tide in March 1931. At the time, the sloop had been fitted with one of the first diesel engines (an Ellwe) to be installed on an inland waterway craft on the Humber and the sailing gear was being kept in situ until the crew developed confidence in the engine. The coal would be discharged at Ben Foster's coalyard on the haven and, as well as these fortnightly deliveries, the Fosters also used *Zenitha* to carry bricks to Hull and Grimsby from their own yards at Barrow Haven, New Holland and on the Ancholme. Additionally, they kept these yards supplied with coal from Fryston, near Castleford. The sailing gear was eventually sold in 1933 and the vessel itself sold for bank stoning in 1946. (*Hull Maritime Museum*)

Above: Craft were able to come up Barton Haven as far as the railway station on spring tides. On this 1931 view looking north, a wooden sloop is shown discharging coal by barrow and basket across the road (Waterside) into Ben Foster's coal yard at low water when the haven had almost dried out. (*Hull Maritime Museum*)

Right: A wooden sloop is shown discharging coal using mast and derrick together with baskets and barrows at Greenwoods' brickyard on the eastern bank of Barton Haven below the ropeworks. The ropery closed in 1989. (*Hull Maritime Museum*)

A view looking out into the Humber from a point west of Barton Haven towards the Farmers' Co. jetty as the sloop *Sprite*, built in 1910 by Warrens of New Holland for James Barraclough & Co. of Hull, is shown heading light downriver in the 1940s. *Sprite* was the last sloop to trade under sail on the Humber before being unrigged in 1950 and converted to a lighter. The sloop heading for the mouth of the haven is Stamps' market boat *Rosalie Stamp* which was motorised in the 1950s, by which time the service had fallen to two or three sailings each way per week. (*Cyril Harrison Collection*)

The Barton sloop *Paradise* is shown grounded at low water on Paull Sands, on the Humber's north bank, below Hull in the 1920s or 1930s. Sand is being loaded into panniers to be carried up planks and dumped in the vessel's hold by a gang of casual labourers. These 'Paull Sanders' would then float off with the tide and deliver their cargoes to the many south bank brick and tile yards where it would be used for many purposes in the manufacturing processes. (*Roger Foster Collection*)

Whitakers' tug *Cawood* towed five empty lighters downriver from Selby in the ice of January 1963. Off Barton, a towrope made brittle by the heavy frost, snapped and, in turning on a stormy Humber to recover the drifting craft, the tug was holed by the anchor of one of them and sank 200yds from the bank. The mate managed to swim/float ashore with the aid of an oil drum and raised the alarm, but two of *Cawood*'s crew were lost. Subsequently, the former Trent Navigation Co.'s towing barge *Frank Rayner* passed over the sunken vessel, causing damage to the tug's wheelhouse as shown on this picture taken after recovery of the tug and its return to Hull Harbour.

Six
The Humber Bridge and Ferriby Cliffs

PROPOSED HUMBER BRIDGE

Drawing of bridge which the experts have suggested should be erected over the Humber between Barton and Hessle.

Proposals for road and/or rail crossings of the Humber began in the late nineteenth century and involved tunnels beneath the water as well as bridges above it. These continued into the twentieth century and the illustration shows an artist's impression of a road bridge planned in 1929 and accepted by Parliament. Because the Government's offer of a grant of seventy-five per cent of the cost was later withdrawn due to the financial situation at the time, it was not built. The view from the south bank shows a vessel heading downriver beneath the 900ft span over the navigation channel.

Work on the present Humber Bridge began in 1972 after the Government, encouraged by an impending local by-election, offered to lend seventy-five per cent of the cost of the project. The photograph shows the Barton side of the bridge as boatmen saw it from the river in 1978 when its main cables were being spun.

The Humber Bridge, completed in 1981.

Opposite, below: Humber Bridge road deck sections were assembled at Priory Yard, Hessle, about a mile downstream of the bridge site. They were then loaded onto pontoons and pushed upstream to beneath their respective positions on the bridge. The first section to be lifted and hung over the river was placed in position in November 1979 to be followed by sections either side of it. This picture, taken in April 1980, shows British Waterways' push tug *Freight Pioneer* setting off for the Barton side with a section loaded onto the pontoon from the gantry outside its construction site. *Leslene*, the bridge run-about boat, on which a few former Barton sloopmen worked, lies moored in the foreground. The 124th and final section was lifted into place in July 1980.

This view from Hessle foreshore across to the Barton side of the Humber Bridge dates from 1997. It shows a gravel barge heading upriver from Hull on the 'first of flood', four hours before high water, bound for a wharf above Gainsborough to load another cargo of Trent aggregate.

The pedestrian ways across the Humber Bridge afford excellent vantage points for photographing river traffic. Here, the former petroleum tanker barge *Battle Stone*, with the graveller *Marnham* fastened alongside, is pictured from the eastern walkway in 2002, bound to load aggregate on the Trent.

HUMBERSIDE INDUSTRY.
LOADING TILES AT A BARTON BRICKYARD.

A seagoing vessel is shown beached at the wooden jetty outside William Blyth's brick and tile works west of Barton and the Humber Bridge for pantiles to be loaded by barrow and plank. Workmen took tiles up the far plank and returned with empty barrows down the nearer slope. The many water-filled pits, now converted for leisure use, bear testimony to the activities of these companies.

ANNIE MAUD.

Above: A ship is shown heading down the Humber in the early 1950s past the short wooden jetty at Chowder (Chalder) Ness. A depth indicator, illuminated at night, at the end of the jetty was vital to shipping on this part of the Humber before the days of radar and automatic sounding equipment. A fog horn was also fitted to the jetty.

Left: James Barraclough & Co.'s sloop *Annie Maud* often carried stone from Ferriby Cliffs down the Humber to Spurn to be used in bank protection work.

Sloops are shown at anchor off Ferriby Cliffs in the 1900s waiting to load limestone, probably from Leggott's Jetty. Crews have used their cog boats to go ashore.

In addition to limestone's use for bank stoning, chalk, a slightly different textured but chemically identical mineral, from quarries between Barton and South Ferriby was ground to make whiting used in the manufacture of polish, paint, pharmaceuticals and putty. The latter was the major use at Thwaite Mill alongside the Aire & Calder Navigation, near Leeds in the early 1950s when James Barraclough & Co.'s former sloop *Rhoda B* was photographed in the snow, having delivered the mineral from Leggott's Jetty, below Ferriby Cliff. Thwaite Mill was closed in the 1970s after floods destroyed the nearby weir, leaving the waterwheels that powered the mill machinery high and dry.

Left: The HKSPS's 61½ft x 15½ft sailing sloop *Amy Howson* is shown beached in 1980 at Chequers, near the site of Leggott's Jetty, on the Humber foreshore below Ferriby Cliffs. This permitted general inspection below its waterline and allowed black varnish to be applied the hull. The vessel was built in 1914 at Beverley as the keel *Sophia* and renamed *Amy Howson* in 1924 after purchase by W.H. Barraclough & Co., by which time it had been converted to a sloop. *Amy* was eventually motorised and, in 1976, purchased by the Humber Keel and Sloop Preservation Society before being re-rigged as a sloop. (*Les Reid*)

Right: Seen in 2002, the distant coaster *Hoo Swift*, having made a ninety-degree turn at the light float shown off Ferriby Cliff, follows the navigation channel to the north of Read's Island as it heads up the Humber with a cargo for one of the Trent wharves.

Seven
The Ancholme Navigation

This view looks downstream from the head of the Ancholme Navigation at Bishopbridge, nineteen miles from the Humber, where, in the 1920s, a small keel has just discharged its cargo to a cart using the hand crane adjacent to the Farmers' Co. warehouse. The wharf was used in the nineteenth century by farmers for miles around for all their imports and exports. In the twentieth century, fertilisers and cattle cake were the major imports but there was little activity after the outbreak of the Second World War.

In September 1978, before a new mast had been acquired for the vessel, the Humber Keel and Sloop Preservation Society took *Amy Howson* as far as they could up the long and straight 'new' River Ancholme. Harlam Hill Lock, where the photograph was taken, was the furthest point reached as it was too narrow to permit *Amy* to pen through. Before the Second World War, there was a little traffic in coal up to this part of the navigation with craft often returning with sand collected from the Ancholme/Rase confluence nearby. (*Les Reid*)

For over half a century, until taken over by another company in the 1910s, Fox's market boat took both goods and passengers from Brandy Wharf to Brigg market, and back, every Thursday, stopping en route at the landings encountered. By the time this picture was taken in the mid-1990s, the warehouse where agricultural cargoes, including sugar beet, were formerly handled had been converted to apartments and the Ancholme had become the preserve of pleasure boaters and fishermen. The photographer's trailboat *Schandelle* is shown heading downstream towards the small settlement, having been launched into the water using the pub's slipway on the opposite bank, partly obscured by the tree. (*John Lower*)

Opened about 1800 and abandoned in 1855, having only reached a point four miles from the town to the east, giving the waterway its name, the four-mile long Caistor Canal joined the Ancholme about a mile below Brandy Wharf. This picture, taken from the Ancholme floodbank, shows the remains of Beck End Lock, the westernmost of five locks constructed on the waterway. Coal and lime were imported to the canal's terminal basin at Moortown and agricultural produce exported from it during the waterway's short life. Its demise was hastened when the MS & LR opened a railway station halfway between Moortown and Caistor in 1848.

A new and straighter course which avoided Brigg town centre was cut for the Ancholme in the seventeenth century. A sugar processing factory was built in 1928 on the new channel's western bank above the town. It received its first waterborne cargo in April 1929 when craft including Furley & Co.'s keel *Loxley* and James Barraclough & Co.'s motor barge *A Triumph* brought a consignment of Cuban sugar over from Hull. The craft are shown moored across river from the factory waiting to discharge their cargoes. (*Valerie and John Holland Collection*)

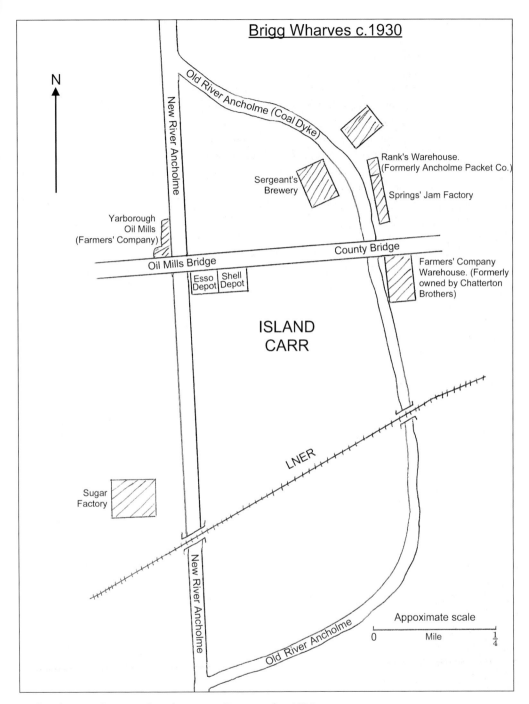

A sketch map showing the wharves at Brigg in the 1930s.

Sacks of imported raw sugar are shown being lifted out of A *Triumph* and transferred to railway wagons on the sugar factory sidings; an extra and expensive movement which probably explains why the factory's involvement with water transport lasted for only twenty years. Craft were also used to deliver home-grown sugar beet here; that from mid-Lincolnshire farms coming down the Ancholme whilst that from Trentside sources coming upriver via the Humber and Ferriby Sluice. (*J. Cairns Collection per Bernard Hughes*)

Opposite, above: In the mid-1920s, both the Shell and Anglo-American (later Esso) petroleum companies built depots on the eastern bank of the new river above the road bridge at Brigg and this upstream view shows craft, including Esso's *Fossgate* and Harkers' *Daphne H*, moored at the nearby petrol jetty in June 1953. *Fossgate* brought the first cargo to the Anglo-American Oil Co.'s depot in October 1925, along with their *Tetney* (see page 22), which also delivered to Barton Haven. Both craft continued to work to Brigg until the 1950s. Despite being plastered from stem to stern with notices such as 'No Smoking', 'No Naked Lights', 'Highly Inflammable' etc. *Fossgate's* engine was started by playing three huge blow-lamp flames onto the cylinder heads until they were hot enough to combust the fuel.

Opposite, below: Looking downstream from the bridge, a queue of loaded sailing craft may be seen waiting to discharge their cargoes of coal or seeds for crushing at Yarborough Oil Mills, built in the late nineteenth century. The mills were owned at the time (1900s) by the Farmers' Co., founded in 1874, who advertised themselves as 'manufacturers of chemical manures, linseed and oil cake and seed crushers'. The mills were served mainly by sloops owned by a different Barraclough: W.H. Barraclough & Co., a subsidiary of the Farmers' Co.

95

A fire in 1910 led to rebuilding of the mills and, until the Second World War, linseed and cottonseed were brought to Yarborough Mills by water for crushing, but by the 1960s, fishmeal, maize and soyabean meal were delivered only for storage, and this finished in 1971. A motor barge identified as *Amy Howson* is shown discharging a cargo in these latter years using the modern hoist. (*J.H. Boyes*)

Opposite, above: Most wharves in central Brigg were situated below County Bridge and were effectively on a loop of the old Ancholme course off the staightened river. This was called the Coal Dyke because coal for the gasworks, Springs' jam factory and private coal merchants was discharged here. This upstream view dates from the 1900s and shows a keel moored at A.M. & E. Sergeant & Co.'s brewery wharf. In addition to being brewers and maltsters, Sergeants were also coal merchants.

Opposite, below: Looking upstream on the Coal Dyke towards Brigg's County Bridge, James Barraclough & Co.'s *Mabel* may be seen moored close to the camera. The Farmers' Co.'s steam keel *Swift*, built in 1894 by Joseph Scarr of Beverley, lies tied up outside the Ancholme Packet Co.'s warehouse on the opposite side of the waterway. The photograph was taken after 1907 when the Farmers' Co. had bought the warehouse beyond the bridge from the Chatterton Brothers who owned both it and *Swift* when the previous picture was taken. *Swift* brought cargoes beneath the bridge to the warehouse until the vessel was sold in 1920.

Opposite, above: Ranks' Hull premises were situated as shown, alongside the eastern side of the harbour at Drypool Bridge. Regular cargoes of flour for Brigg originated here, to be discharged on the Coal Dyke.

Opposite, below: A scene in the 1940s off Keadby on the River Trent as the coaster *Grit* and 1896-built wooden sloop *John and Annie*, with leeboard lowered, arrive to load coal. The former vessel would probably be bound for the Thames after loading. *John and Annie*, purchased by John Frank & Sons in 1934, would load from railway wagons at a staithe a short distance along the Stainforth & Keadby Canal. It would then deliver its cargo to Brigg gashouse, having carried one load of coal in the summer and two in winter there each week from the early years of the twentieth century when it was owned by Walt Burkill.

The Ancholme Packet Co. ran market boats from Brigg to Hull thrice weekly after its formation in 1879, calling at landings en route. This picture dating from 1911, shows cargo being discharged from or loaded onto their steam barge *Togo*. The company were taken over by Ranks, the millers, in the 1920s.

A wooden keel heads up the Ancholme above Coal Dyke end, below Brigg, in the 1900s with both mainsail and topsail raised. Cargo is being transhipped from the moored vessel beyond into an adjacent lighter for carriage further up the navigation.

Opposite, above: The iron sailing keel *Voluta*, built by Warrens in 1908, is coming down the Ancholme in 1932 after delivering a cargo to Brigg. The vessel brought many cargoes of flour from Ranks' mills at Hull to the former Ancholme Packet Co. warehouse and also carried cattle cake to the warehouse from premises on the River Hull.

Opposite, below: In its drainage function, the Ancholme was regarded for many years as being in need of dredging. The dredger *Ancholme* was built in Holland for work on the river and arrived at South Ferriby in 1935 where it began work in mid-September and finished two years later at the southern end of the navigation. The vessel was able to discharge either into barges or onto the banks. It is seen in 1936 after doing the latter, moored above Saxby Bridge, between Brigg and South Ferriby, during a run-off of the river.

Bridges crossing the Ancholme Navigation all differ markedly from each other, though all sailing craft had to lower their masts and sails to pass beneath them. Horkstow Suspension Bridge, shown here looking downstream, has a main span of 134ft and was completed in 1836 to a design by Sir John Rennie.

In 1900, when this photograph was taken, the sloop *John and Annie* was owned by Walt Burkill and is in use here to bring coal to its subsequent owners, the 1870-established brickmakers John Frank & Sons who had premises lining the eastern bank of the Ancholme between the Horkstow boundary and Ferriby Sluice. The vessel was also used to take away finished bricks to Hull or Grimsby as well as to bring coal to Brigg gasworks. Coal was also carried to a steam-powered pumping station at Cadney Bridge, 2½ miles above Brigg, vessels loading ten tonnes less than for the brickyards or gasworks to compensate for the shallow draught above Brigg.

If bricks were being loaded aboard, the sails would be tied up as shown, lee-boards lowered onto the riverbed to keep the vessel steady, and a plank placed across from the vessel to the wharfside. Three men would then wheel bricks aboard, fifty at a time, whilst one man stowed the cargo. In this manner, about 4,000 bricks were loaded in an hour, 30,000 a day. Franks were extensive users of the waterways for imports of coal and export of bricks, railways never having reached South Ferriby. The last Franks' yard to close was in 1962, beaten by red tape and economics.

Opposite, below: Water sports were an annual event at several places on the Humber waterways and here, at Ferriby Sluice, they continued until about 1928. The Greasy Pole competition is shown in progress and someone in fancy dress has managed to walk out almost to within grabbing distance of the flag at its end. The pole was a yacht boom, sanded smooth, free from splits and well greased, projecting out over the water from a vessel moored to the bank. One of John Frank & Sons' brick kilns lies in the background with piles of bricks visible.

Nero, was owned by John Frank & Sons from new in 1896 when it became the last vessel to be built by Henry Scarr at Beverley before he moved to Hessle. For over fifty years, the iron sloop, 61½ ft x 15½ ft, was a familiar sight on the Ancholme and Humber. It is shown here on the Ancholme near Ferriby Sluice shortly after being sold by Franks, around 1950. The vessel had been engined and a wheelhouse was added before the Second World War. Buckets crossing the waterway carried chalk from quarries to the east to the cement works built on the west bank in the late 1930s.

Harkers' tanker *Sabina H* was specially built for the Brigg trade as a dumb barge and made its first visit to the Ancholme in February 1929. The vessel loaded at Saltend and came to Brigg as described on page 2. The tanker was motorised in the 1930s and is shown here heading upriver after leaving the lock at Ferriby Sluice in 1950. By this time petrol had given way to aviation fuel bound for Lincolnshire's many RAF airfields. *Sabina H* brought the final cargo to the oil company depots in September 1958.

The tankers *Veracitie*, *Sabina H*, and *Birkdale H* are shown halted by the ice at Ferriby Sluice in 1954 whilst bound for Brigg. Notice the large pieces of ice broken by the craft to get alongside the quay wall. Under normal conditions, the skipper of *Birkdale H* was notorious for producing a wave 4ft high behind him which swept over the towpath washing anglers off their baskets. Sometimes, he postponed his river runs to Sundays to catch more fishermen and, even if he failed to get the men, he managed to suck the water away from them and drag keep nets from their pegs.

Starting in 1856 and lasting for fifty years, the passenger boat provided a service between Bishopthorpe, later Brigg, and Ferriby Sluice to connect with the ferry to Hull. The vessel is shown in Ferriby Lock in the 1890s.

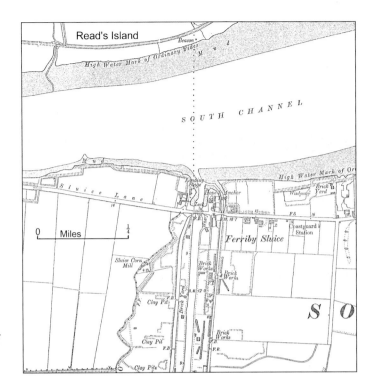

Right: A 1908 OS map of the area surrounding Ferriby Sluice.

On a dark February night in 1935, in a rush to lower the sails as *Amy Howson* entered the lock at Ferriby Sluice from the Humber, the mate failed to hang a stop rope on the lock bollard. The sloop collided with the old cast-iron swing bridge across the lock on which lock-keeper Frank Straw is shown standing in 1933. A 6ft x 1½ft part of one of the girders was broken off resulting in a new replacement bridge being installed later that year. This bridge in turn was replaced in 1983. The Hope and Anchor is visible in the background together with an old barge wheelhouse on the lockside which had become the lock-keeper's hut.

Some vessels were too long to pen through the 78ft x 19ft lock at Ferriby Sluice normally, but could pass through with gates open at both ends when the Ancholme and Humber 'made a level'. Only one oversize vessel up to 84ft in length was allowed to pass in each direction on one tide. G.D. Holmes' *Semloh*, with a name derived from its owner's which also served as the company's telegraphic address, was one such craft. *Semloh* had been lengthened in the 1940s from its original 61½ ft to enable it to carry more cargo on the Fossdyke to Saxilby, near Lincoln. This vessel is shown, together with *Colwick*, crossing Goole's West Dock after loading overside from a ship. *Greendale* (see page 50) was also too long to pen through the lock and, similarly made several voyages to Brigg.

Above: This 1900s downstream view of the lock and sluices at South Ferriby shows the replacement sluices and road bridge built in 1903. A new road bridge across the sluices was constructed in 1935. Navigation often took second place to drainage on the Ancholme. Local farmers were extremely vociferous and well-connected and the sluices were opened in times of flood whenever the Ancholme water level was above that in the Humber, thereby draining much valuable farmland. It was also customary to drain the river during two weeks each spring in order to clean, repair and tar all the sluice doors and examine the various workings which would normally be underwater. Barge traffic could not move upriver against the flow on these 'run-offs' and if a vessel came down at this time it was virtually out of control. Numerous accidents have happened and several encounters between sluice and craft have been prevented by a vigilant lock-keeper at South Ferriby who closed the sluices for a few minutes whilst the crews of craft coming downstream regained control of their vessels and tied them up.

Right: Hargreaves' motor barge *Evelynston*, having brought West Yorkshire coal to the nearby cement works, is moored inside Ferriby Sluice during a run-off in the late 1930s, waiting to load cement for the return voyage.

The sailing keel *Olga*, seen here sailing down the Sheffield & South Yorkshire Navigation at Thorne, was one of the vessels to fall foul of the sluices at Ferriby when, in 1933, it broke adrift during a run-off and came rushing downriver. Despite the crew managing to get ropes ashore, these parted one by one and *Olga* went through the west sluice, breaking away the sluice gate platform and chains.

Eight

Ferriby Sluice to the Ouse/Trent Confluence

Sloops are shown waiting at the packet jetty with sails set as high water approaches before setting off down to Hull. Stamps' *Burgate* is the light vessel whilst the loaded craft were owned by James Barraclough & Co and are, from left: *Peggy*, *John William* and *Rhoda B*. The company also owned some motor barges but ceased trading in 1975.

Opposite, above: Sailing vessels wishing to be towed to and from the Ancholme Navigation at Ferriby Sluice and those craft without sails used steam or diesel powered tugs for the voyage. The United Towing Co., formed by an amalgamation of Hull tug owners in 1921, provided the service and most of their fleet is shown on this 1930 photograph taken at Hull.

Opposite, below: From 1925, Franks' *Nero* had a cog boat with a 4hp outboard motor clamped onto it for moving the sloop out into the Humber or assisting it when becalmed in the estuary. It is shown in use here to push the vessel, loaded with bricks and probably destined for Williamsons' wharf above North Bridge on the Harbour at Hull, away from Ferriby Lock.

Below the lock and sluices at South Ferriby there was yet another floating dry dock; this one owned by Richard Leggott. New planking is being spiked onto its occupant's existing planks; a cheaper repair option than re-planking onto the vessel's frames.

Bricks from the Ancholme are here being discharged by hand from a sloop in Queen's Dock, Hull in the 1920s. They were also off-loaded in this manner further up the harbour and in Grimsby Docks.

John Richardson & Son's steel sloop *Skelfleet* was built at Howdendyke in 1924 by T.H. Scarr & Son and converted from sail to power by installation of an Ellwe engine in the 1930s. The vessel is shown, shortly after conversion, outside H. Williamson & Co.'s wharf on the river Hull above North Bridge where it delivered millions of bricks from south bank wharves. These were discharged, 250 at a time, on boards, using a steam crane.

Bullocks, having spent the summer grazing on Read's Island, are shown on this poor photograph being transferred back to the mainland near the old Hope and Anchor at Ferriby Sluice in the autumn. The animals were almost wild and moved about the hold during the voyage, making the vessel with anything less than a full cargo very difficult to control. This was also the case when only a few sheep or cattle were being moved prior to being taken to market, or when two or three horses were being transported. The ramp for the animals between deck and hold is visible to the left of the picture. The sloop used, *Providence*, eventually became so rat-infested that it was burnt up on the island. After the Second World War, a motorised ex-landing craft was used to transport the animals.

Ferriby Sluice and Haven are shown on this aerial photograph, dating from 1949, looking north towards the Humber. The Sloop Inn, demolished in 1969, is partly visible in the right foreground. Craft waiting for the tide are tied up at the 'packet jetty' which was removed in 1973 by Lincoln & Hull Marine Contractors who cut off the piles down to mud level. They had to return and repeat the exercise after the next run-off which washed away much of the mud leaving remains of the piles standing proud.

The Goole & Hull Steam Packet Co.'s paddle steamer *Her Majesty*, used on the Hull-Ferriby ferry service before the First World War, and an unknown tug are shown tied up at Ferriby Sluice packet jetty in the 1900s. (*Brian Peeps Collection*)

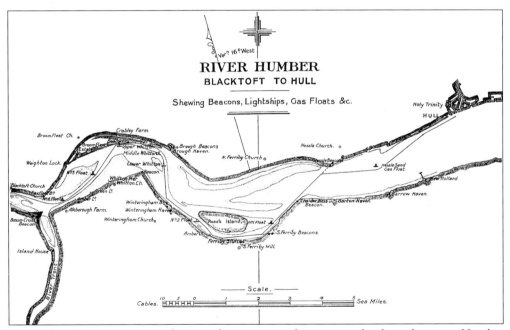

A Humber Conservancy map showing the positions of navigational aids in the upper Humber *c*.1910, when the shipping channel passed south of Read's Island.

Opposite, below: Looking towards Read's Island in the early 1960s, 'Cliff' ships used for stoning Humber, Trent and Ouse banks, and even the Ancholme above Brigg, are shown tied up to Ferriby Sluice Jetty at low water. Stone for this purpose was collected from Leggott's Jetty, below Ferriby Cliff until 1963. The early history of *Zenitha*, the outer vessel, was described on page 76. At times, the main Humber shipping channel passed between Read's Island and Ferriby Sluice but it currently again passes to the north of the island.

Above: For many years, lightships, lighthouses, buoys and beacons have been positioned on or near the Humber to guide vessels on the river. Additionally, eleven gas floats were in use. Gas float No.1 marked the eastern end of Read's Island and No.2 lay to the west of the island. In the days when the navigation channel passed south of the island, between it and the Lincolnshire shore, these were essential for navigation. From 1896 until the Second World War, the lights were serviced by a lighter carrying a gas holder which was taken to Hull gasworks by horse and railway to be filled. On the river, the lighter was handled by the schooner-rigged steam launch *Queen*, as shown, with several floats being charged on each trip.

A coal-fired steam paddle tug owned by the Goole & Hull Steam Towing Co. is shown in the 1900s off Winteringham Haven hauling eight barges in V-formation down the Humber to Hull from Goole. (*HKSPS*)

Above: Two paddle steamers, probably the Goole & Hull Steam Packet Co.'s *Her Majesty* and *Empress*, are shown discharging their passengers at low water onto a landing on the Humber foreshore near Winteringham in 1907. The vessels would most likely be bringing visitors from Hull to the annual village show. (*Brian Peeps Collection*)

Opposite, below: Harkers' tanker barge *Baysdale H*, inexplicably found itself aground on Read's Island whilst coming down the Humber light in the early 1950s. With the Humber Conservancy's approval, the company's diesel tug *Lion* flushed away part of the island enabling the vessel to be refloated at high water.

Until the Second World War, there was a weekly market boat between Winteringham Haven and Hull. This view dates from the 1900s and features a seagoing vessel occupying Routh & Waddingham's floating dry dock in the haven.

Routh & Waddingham's boatyard in Winteringham Haven is shown in the 1920s on this view looking north with a wooden vessel under construction and another contained in the company's barely visible floating dry dock. Until the Second World War coal was loaded in the haven from railway wagons and delivered to Brigg and brickyards at Broomfleet on the Market Weighton Canal, sited on the north bank of the Humber. The haven is now one of the bases of the Humber Yawl Club.

Right: Faxfleet and other sloops owned by John Richardson & Son are shown in the 1920s moored on the Market Weighton Canal. The craft delivered coal to, and carried bricks from, works at Broomfleet Landing, a couple of miles up the canal. The coal was loaded to barge at a wharf on Winteringham Haven, just out of shot to the left of the previous photograph. It had been carried from Scunthorpe in wagons along the North Lindsey Light Railway. The railway, sponsored by the GCR, was opened to Winteringham in 1910. *Faxfleet* was the only wooden vessel in the six-strong Richardson fleet of sloops (*Marfleet, Ousefleet, Brickfleet, Faxfleet, Skelfleet* and *Swinefleet*) and had the distinction of winning the final three Barton sloop races in 1927, 1928 and 1929.

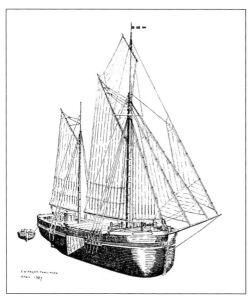

Left: This drawing by Edward Paget-Tomlinson depicts the billyboy *Aimwell* built in 1883 at Winteringham. (See also page 11)

This view across the Humber towards Brough from the mouth of Winteringham Haven shows the extensive and uneven muddy sands which bare out at low water in the upper Humber and pose problems for any vessel unfortunate enough to become stranded on them.

Opposite, above: Seagoing vessels and inland waterway craft have experienced difficulties in this area of the upper Humber, both on the north and south banks. Several vessels have capsized, broken their backs or failed to rise with the tide after grounding on the sandy and uneven riverbed. Fortunately, the steam tug *Autocrat* which ran into difficulties and sank off Whitton Church in July 1934 was able to be rescued by the craft shown, which included other United Towing Co. tugs.

Right: Whitton Jetty was built just west of the village in the mid-nineteenth century as a calling point for the Hull-Gainsborough steam packets. Nearby was a 40yd-long narrow gauge railway running along the Humber foreshore to move the lower of two navigation lights in the vicinity as the sandbanks shifted, so that when a vessel was in the navigation channel, the upper light appeared to be immediately above the lower one. The jetty was demolished in the 1920s and little trace of it remains.
(*Brian Peeps Collection*)

Two motor barges owned by British Oil and Cake Mills head up the Humber off Whitton in 1979 loaded with oil seeds imported via Hull bound for their owner's Ouse-side crushing-mills at Selby.

This 2002 photograph was taken from Grid Reference SE883235 just off the Alkborough-Whitton road looking across Broomfleet Island to Weighton lock on the north bank. The farmland called Alkborough Flats lies in the foreground and the loaded Trent graveller heading downriver to Hull is almost certainly *Joyce Hawksley*.

The wooden clinker-built keel *Hannah and Harriet* is shown in the late 1890s at anchor in an area known to boatmen as Walker Dykes. This part of the Humber lies close to the western end of the high ground between Whitton and Trent Falls, adjacent to the farmland of Alkborough Flats. This was a comfortable and safe place for small unpowered inland waterway craft trading between Hull and Trent ports or the Sheffield & South Yorkshire Navigation to wait for the tide, whether moving upriver or down. I was given this print by Mrs Evelyn Holt whose father, William Pattrick, owned the vessel. She described her mother's honeymoon trip on the keel from Denaby to Hull in the 1880s when a trawler collided with the vessel causing her mother to fall against the tiller, knocking her unconscious.

Left: Construction of Apex light at the Ouse/Trent confluence in the 1930s is shown as the training walls on both rivers were nearing completion.

Below: This 2002 view across the Humber from Faxfleet Ness on the north bank shows John Dean's tug *Shovette* pushing a LASH barge (see page 45) past Apex light as it leaves the Humber bound for Grove Wharf on the Trent with a cargo of imported steel. Alkborough and its church tower may also be seen.

Craft leave their berths to head for the sea as soon as there is sufficient water in the river for them to navigate safely. Here, in 2002, by the time of high water at Trent Falls, *Magic* is coming down the Ouse from Goole after delivering shea nuts from the Ivory Coast of West Africa. At the same time another light outward-bound seagoing vessel, just visible near its bows, heads down the Trent from Grove Wharf.

This magnificent aerial view of the area known as Trent Falls was kindly provided by the Associated British Ports' Harbourmaster at Hull. It shows the confluence of the Rivers Trent (left) and Ouse to form the Humber. Tempus Publishing have featured the Trent in their *The River Trent Navigation* and the Ouse in *The Yorkshire Ouse Navigation*. The new Apex light shown was installed at the end of the 1990s. (*ABP*)